MERCURY
AND THE SUN

MERCURY AND THE SUN

Duncan Brewer

MARSHALL CAVENDISH
NEW YORK · LONDON · TORONTO · SYDNEY

Reference Edition Published 1993

© Marshall Cavendish Corporation 1992

Published by Marshall Cavendish Corporation
2415 Jerusalem Avenue
PO Box 587
North Bellmore
New York 11710

Series created by Graham Beehag Book Design

Library of Congress Cataloging-in-Publication Data

Brewer, Duncan, 1938-
   Mercury / Duncan Brewer.
      p. cm. — (Planet guides)
   Summary: Examines the physical characteristics and conditions of Mercury, describing its position in relation to the sun and other planets and surveying humanity's attempts to penetrate its mysteries.
   ISBN 1-85435-368-3 (set) ISBN 1-85435-369-1
   1. Mercury (Planet) — Juvenile literature. [1. Mercury (Planet)]
   I. Title. II. Series: Brewer, Duncan, 1938- Planet guides.
   QB611.B74 1990   90-40807
                                                                  CIP
                                                                   AC

Printed in Malaysia by Times Offset Pte Ltd

SAFETY NOTE

Never look directly at the Sun, either with the naked eye or with binoculars or a telescope. To do so can result in permanent blindness.

Acknowledgement

Most of the photographs, maps and diagrams in this book have been kindly supplied by NASA.

Title Page Picture:
The Mariner 10 spacecraft obtained this view of Mercury during its out-going pass on March 29, 1974. This photomosaic has been tinted to approximate the visual appearance of Mercury.

Contents

Mercury

Mercury, the closest planet to the Sun, is hot and hasty. Just 36,000,000 miles (57,900,000 kilometers) from the Sun on average, Mercury hurtles around its parent star at a breakneck 105,600 mph (170,000 km/h). If it went any slower, the Sun's massive gravitational pull would drag it to blazing extinction.

Mariner 10 made three fly-bys mapping Mercury in 1974 and 1975. They revealed a similar surface to that of the Moon. Mariner 10 photographed about 45 percent of Mercury's surface.

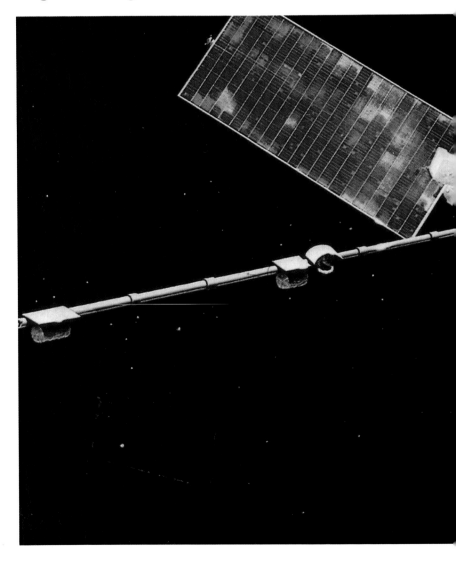

Although Mercury is surrounded by a thin layer of helium gas, there is so little of it that the amount collected from a 4 mile (6·4 km) diameter sphere would be just enough to fill a child's balloon.

Two in One

Ancient stargazers thought that Mercury was two different heavenly bodies. Sometimes it appears on one side of the Sun, like a second morning star. At other times, it appears on the other side, as a secondary evening star. Just as the morning and evening stars are

both the planet Venus, so the two secondary "stars" are Mercury. When Mercury appeared in the evening, the Greeks called it Hermes. When it appeared in the morning, they called it Apollo. The Egyptians called it Set and Horus.

Not all early astronomers agreed. Around 350 B.C., Heraclides of Pontus calculated that Mercury and Venus traveled around the Sun. This would explain why these two planets, which were closer to the Sun than the Earth, appeared first on one side of it, and then on the other. In the following century, Aristarchus of Samos agreed with Heraclides. He even proposed that all planets, including Earth, orbited the Sun. However, these revolutionary ideas were not acceptable to most Greeks. They preferred the philosophical "proof" expounded by another Greek, Aristotle. He believed that Earth was the center of the universe.

Hide and Seek

Mercury is only about one fiftieth as bright as Venus, and because it stays so close to the Sun, it is the most difficult planet for us to see. This is particularly true in places where evening and morning skies are frequently obscured by clouds. Even some famous astronomers never saw Mercury. One of them was Copernicus, who in the sixteenth century developed the theory that the Earth orbited the Sun, like the other planets. He was

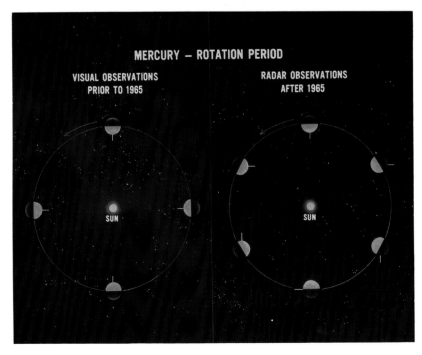

In 1965 new radar techniques forced astronomers to revise their views on Mercury's rotation speed. The planet was once thought always to present the same face to the Sun. We now know that it rotates on its own axis three times in the course of every two orbits of the Sun.

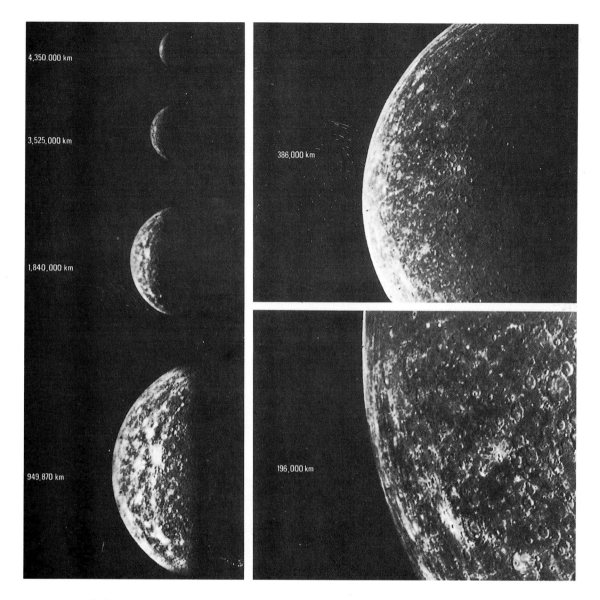

4,350,000 km

3,525,000 km

1,840,000 km

949,870 km

386,000 km

196,000 km

prevented from viewing Mercury by river mists in his home region in Poland.

Even after the introduction of telescopes in the seventeenth century, Mercury remained relatively unknown. Its small diameter 3,047 miles (4,900 kilometers), only a third that of the Earth, and its closeness to the Sun's glare, made it hard to see.

Seen with the naked eye from Earth, Mercury and Venus behave similarly, although Mercury never rises as high in the sky as its neighbor. At the most, Mercury climbs about a quarter of the way to the *zenith* (the point in the sky directly over the head of the observer). Mercury never falls more than about 11½

Sequences of Mariner 10 photographs, taken as the space probe approached Mercury in 1974, show a surface covered in impact craters. The largest is the Caloris Basin. Mariner 10 went "off the air" on March 24, 1975, but is still orbiting the Sun.

hours behind the Sun, whether it is rising or setting.

Today's city dwellers are surrounded by street lighting that effectively cancels out the soft, subtle light of dusk and dawn. So they hardly ever get the chance to see Mercury unless they go to the countryside – or have a power cut.

Until 1965, astronomers believed that Mercury kept the same face turned permanently toward the Sun, in the same way that the Moon keeps the same face turned toward the Earth. They calculated that Mercury's rotation period on its own *axis* was 88 Earth days, the same time that it takes to orbit the Sun.

The Long Day

In 1965, using the 1,000-foot (305-meter) dish of the huge Arecibo *radio telescope* in Puerto Rico, a team of astronomers bounced strong radio pulses off Mercury and analyzed the echoes. Their calculations proved that Mercury had a rotation of 58·65 Earth days. This is two-thirds of its orbital time of 87·97 Earth days. A "day" from sunrise to sunset on Mercury lasts 176 Earth days, and the planet circles the Sun twice in the course of it. Scientists have calculated that Mercury is very dense for its size. It has a heavy metallic core larger in proportion to its overall size than that of any other *terrestrial planet*. Earth's density is the highest in the Solar System, at 12,170 pounds per cubic yard (5,520 kilograms per cubic meter), but Earth has a large mass, and strong gravity to compress its interior.

Heavy Core

Mercury's density is 11,990 pounds per cubic yard (5,440 kilograms per cubic meter). This is the same as saying that it is 5·44 times as dense as water. Physicists used to think that Mercury consisted of a high proportion of dense materials because it is close to the heat of the Sun. They speculated that when the planet formed, only the most heat resistant elements could have

Did You Know?

Mercury, Venus and Mars, along with the Earth, form a group of four rocky planets. They are known as the inner planets because they are the nearest to the Sun.

The radio telescope at Arecibo in Puerto Rico – the largest of its kind. Built in a natural hollow in the ground, it cannot be steered, but its aerial is movable and gives the telescope considerable range.

avoided vaporization in the Sun's heat. The heaviest elements would have melted and sunk to the planet's core. That is what had happened in the other terrestrial planets. However, this does not explain why Mercury's core is so large in relation to its total size.

Asteroid Collision

Some scientists think that Mercury used to be much larger, with a thick *mantle* and crust like the Earth. They have a theory that the outer layers were stripped away after a collision with a large *asteroid* during the formation period of the inner Solar System. This impact left Mercury's core with a greatly reduced outer layer. The planet now consists mainly of core, with a thin crust of rocky *silicon.*

Mercury's speed is constantly changing because its orbit is *elliptical.* At *perihelion*, when the planet is at its closest to the Sun, 28,500,000 miles (45,865,000 kilometers) separate them. At *aphelion*, when Mercury is farthest from the Sun, the distance is 43,300,000 miles (69,680,000 kilometers).

Reversing the Sun

At perihelion, the planet travels faster than when it is farther out in its orbit, because of the increased pull of the Sun's gravitational field. This has a strange effect. For a short while, the speed of the orbit catches up with, and overtakes, the speed of the planet's spin. To anyone standing on Mercury, it would seem as if

Mariner 10 was launched on a path which used Venus's gravity to slow its speed. That maneuver allowed it to close in on Mercury's elliptical orbit. It collected an immense amount of data about different aspects of both planets.

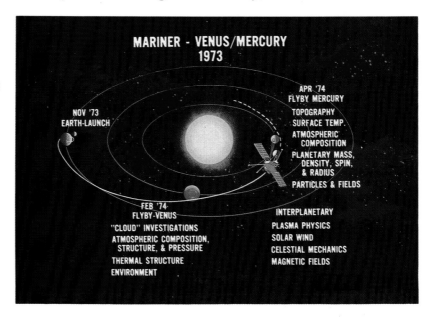

the Sun had slowed down, stopped, and actually gone backward for a while. Then, it would appear to slow down and stop once again, before it resumed its usual trajectory across the sky.

Hot Days and Cold Nights

This slowing and stopping in relation to the Sun means that parts of the planet's surface receive an extra dose of the Sun's radiated energy. At perihelion, the region which gets extra exposure receives about ten times the amount of solar energy experienced by the Moon. The surface temperature at Mercury's equator can reach 660°F (350°C), which is hot enough to melt certain metals.

Mercury, like the Moon, gains and loses heat very fast. The time taken to absorb and conduct heat is called "thermal inertia." On the dark side of the planet, the temperature during the long night falls to as low as −275°F (−170°C).

Phases of Mercury

Like the Moon, Mercury displays phases. The planet's disk, as we see it from Earth, changes from full, to crescent, to new, and then back again. Unfortunately for Earth-bound astronomers, the full phase of the cycle occurs when Mercury is on the far side of the Sun from Earth. Mercury is then said to be at *superior conjunction*.

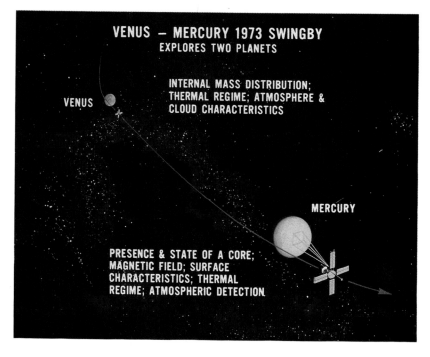

This artist's concept shows the route and exploratory tasks of the Mariner 10 space probe.

Mercury is easiest to see when it is halfway between new and full, at its greatest *elongation*, or separation to the west or east of the Sun. Giovanni Zupus, an Italian astronomer, was the first to notice the phases of Mercury. Using a telescope more powerful than Galileo's, he saw the phases in 1639.

Crossing the Sun

About thirteen times every Earth century, Mercury's orbit brings it directly between the Sun and the Earth, so that we can observe a *transit*. A telescope is needed to see the fast-moving

Controlled from the Canberra Deep Space Station, Mariner 10 made detailed photographs of Mercury's surface during its three fly-bys. The planet's surface proved to consist mainly of igneous silicate rock. The white arrow signifies the swing taken by Mariner 10 as it passed the planet.

planet as a tiny dark disk at its *inferior conjunction*.

Venus also transits the Sun, though less frequently than Mercury. As Venus enters its transit, it moves from dark space into bright light. It has a visible, glowing outline caused by its atmosphere. Mercury displays no luminous ring, for Mercury's atmosphere is extremely thin, almost non-existent. The Sun's intense heat has combined with Mercury's low surface gravity to cause nearly all the gases on the planet to escape. Mariner 10, the only space probe to have visited Mercury, tested the planet for atmosphere on its final encounter in March, 1975. It discovered emissions of helium, neon, and argon, in very small amounts.

Elliptical Orbits

Mercury has the second most *eccentric orbit* of all the planets, after Pluto. In 1609, the German astronomer Johannes Kepler published his "First Law": "Every planet moves around the Sun in an elliptical path, with the Sun as one focus of the *ellipse*." An ellipse is· an oval, or a flattened circle. Instead of having a single center, like a true circle, an ellipse has two centers, or "foci." A line passing through these foci forms the ellipse's major axis. If you draw a straight line from one focus to any point on the circumference of the ellipse, and another straight line from there to the other focus, the combined distance is always the same.

Ellipses can vary in shape from almost circular to flattened cigar shapes. The flatter an ellipse is, the more "eccentric" it is said to be. One way of measuring the eccentricity of an ellipse is to divide the distance between the foci by the length of the major axis. In a circle, there is no distance between the foci. They are identical and form the circle's center. So a true circle has an eccentricity of zero.

If an ellipse is very flat, the distance between its foci is almost the same as the full length of the major axis. Eccentricity varies between zero and almost one. The more eccentric an ellipse, the closer it is to one. Earth's orbit has an eccentricity of 0·017, which is fairly circular. Venus's orbit, with an eccentricity of only 0·007, is very close to circular. Mercury's orbit, however, has an eccentricity of 0·206, making it second in eccentricity to Pluto's, which is 0·25.

Journey to the Innermost Planet

In 1973, NASA launched Mariner 10, which was a spectacular success in surveying Mercury. Mariner 10 blasted off on its 17-month 1,000,000,000 mile (1,600,000,000 kilometer) journey in November, 1973, atop a two-stage Atlas/Centaur rocket carrier. The Atlas first stage accelerated up to 8,000 mph (12,800 km/h) to an altitude of 100 miles (160 kilometers).

This region of Mercury shows a mixture of plains and sharply defined impact craters. Some of the larger craters have younger, smaller craters superimposed on them.

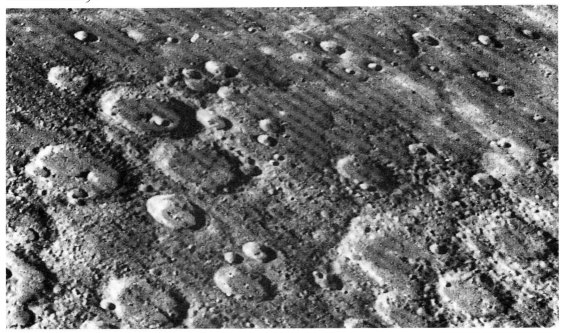

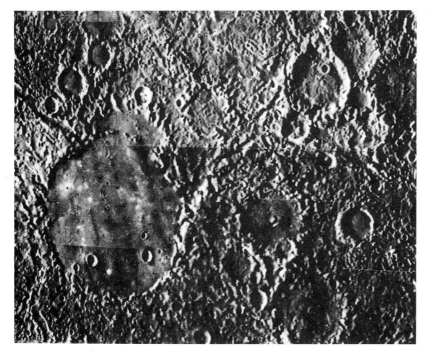

This area of hills, visible among the craters, is unique in the portion of Mercury photographed by Mariner 10. The hills may have been pushed up by massive seismic waves during the formation of the huge Caloris Basin on the other side of the planet.

The Centaur second stage put Mariner into orbit. Then, after staying in orbit for 30 minutes, the rocket boosted the speed of the probe to 25,400 mph (40,875 km/h) aiming it out of Earth's pull on a course for Venus.

The probe then separated from the rocket and emerged like a moth from a chrysalis. It unfurled its instruments and the wide wings of its twin solar panels that were its main source of power.

Rendezvous

One hundred and five days after its launch, Mariner 10

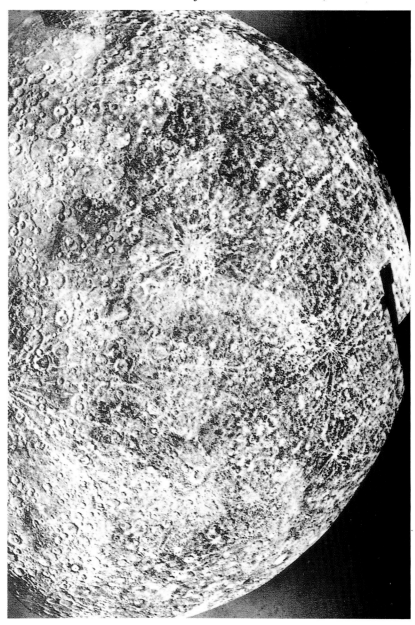

A region near Mercury's south pole displays a profusion of densely packed craters from millions of years of meteoritic impacts. The long scarps, or cliffs, also visible may have been caused by cooling and shrinking in the planet's core.

Ray craters such as this one are thought to be relatively young. The rays probably consist of ejected material thrown out by the meteorite impact which caused the crater.

entered the orbit of Venus at its perihelion. It swung in front of the cloudy planet, and was slowed down by the force of Venus's gravity. Then it was able to rendezvous with Mercury's orbit 53 days later.

Mariner 10 then entered a 176-day orbit of its own around the Sun. This brought it within close striking distance of Mercury every two of the planet's years (176 Earth days). Mariner encountered Mercury three times in all. Minute adjustments to the probe's course were made by its propulsion unit on each occasion. It also stayed in the correct position to allow its instruments to function at their highest efficiency by releasing tiny amounts of nitrogen through special reaction control jets on the solar panels. Throughout its mission, Mariner 10 received instructions from the Canberra Deep Space Station. It relayed back TV images

Some craters show signs of flooding with lava, although there is far less evidence of volcanic activity on Mercury than on the Moon, and the smallest planet lacks the Moon's great smooth "marias," or seas.

as it carried out the mapping of Mercury's hitherto un-known surface.

Sun Protection

Working so close to the Sun, Mariner's instruments had to be protected from fierce radiation. The spacecraft was equipped with an umbrella-like sunshade, as well as many-layered thermal blankets at the top and bottom. Remote-controlled louvered panels, like blinds, were also fitted on five of the vehicle's eight sides.

Darkside Encounter

The first close encounter began on March 29, 1974. Mariner passed over the planet's dark side at an altitude of 435 miles (700 kilometers). Pictures were trans-mitted back to Earth every 42 seconds. A total of 647 images came out of the March rendezvous, though conditions were not ideal for taking pic-tures. The probe was able, on this first encounter, to

Above: Nicknamed the "Teddy Bear," this group of overlapping craters close to the Caloris Basin represents different periods of meteoritic bombardment.

Left: Hun Kal is a small, sharply defined crater, about 1 mile (1·6 kilometers) across, just south of Mercury's equator. Mercury's surface has a higher gravity than the Moon, so the material ejected from impacts does not travel as far as on the Moon.

test Mercury for atmosphere. It also measured the surface temperature of the planet's dark side. In addition, the probe's magnetometers were able to show that Mercury has a slight electromagnetic field.

Coming in Close

The second encounter came in September, 1974, at high altitude, over the sunlit side of the planet. It produced 300 pictures. On its third encounter, in March, 1975, the probe descended to an altitude of only 197 miles (317 kilometers), for a dark-side trajectory at high latitude. This final encounter produced high resolution pictures on which details only 330 feet (100 meters) across could be picked out. The fast-failing Mariner had done its job. Its nitrogen fuel was nearly exhausted, and several of its instruments were going out of commission.

The Scarred Surface

The detailed pictures from Mariner 10 revealed a planetary surface superficially similar to the Moon. Forty percent of Mercury's surface was photographed by the probe. The pictures show a surface closely patterned with the craters of innumerable meteorite impacts. Some of them are very large and are superimposed by later, smaller impact craters. As on the Moon, early lava outpourings filled some of the craters to create smooth surfaces, though this activity ceased more than 3,000,000,000 years ago.

The TV pictures revealed one crater that is truly gigantic. As it is one of Mercury's "hot spots," it was named the Caloris Basin. It has a diameter of 840 miles (1,350 kilometers), with concentric rings of mountains, thrown up as shock waves, extending outward another 625 miles (1,000 kilometers) from the basin's circumference.

The youngest of the impact craters are known as "ray craters." Ray-like streaks radiate out from their centers, passing through and over the craters and crater-walls of earlier impacts.

Shrunken Crust

Mercury's heavy core takes up a disproportionately large part of the planet's volume. Its cooling and shrinking have had a marked effect on the thin mantle. In effect, Mercury's coat has become too big for its body.

The Caloris Basin is the largest feature so far discovered on Mercury. It has a total diameter of 800 miles (1,300 kilometers), including the concentric ridges radiating away from the central basin. The floor of Caloris may be filled with material melted as a result of the enormous impact that created the basin.

The outer skin has become wrinkled and distorted, like the skin of a withered apple.

Unique surface characteristics of Mercury not found on the Moon are the long sinuous ridges known as "lobate scarps." Some of them are 300 miles (483 kilometers) long, and almost two miles (3·2 kilometers) high. They seem to have been caused by the shrinking of the planet's metallic core as it cooled. Some of the core must still be molten: the magnetic field is probably created by rotation currents within the core.

The floor of the Caloris Basin is crisscrossed with fractures and ridges such as these. They may have formed as the planet's interior shrunk, hundreds of millions of years after the crust had solidified.

Mercury and Einstein

Mercury is a long-dead planet that offers no welcome to manned flights or the possibility of space stations. Future space explorers are likely to seek less hostile locations for staging posts further into the galaxy. One day, when other priorities have been met, another probe may try to complete the mapping of this heat-blasted little world.

However, Mercury did play a significant role, early in the twentieth century, in confirming Albert Einstein's revolutionary new theories about the structure of the universe.

Breaking the Rules

In the nineteenth century, the French chemist and astronomer, Urbain Leverrier, discovered that Mercury's orbit was not fully in accord with Newton's Law of Universal Gravitation. It was known that the perihelion point of Mercury's orbit does not stay in the same place in relation to the stars. Instead, it "precesses," or advances very slowly, due to the influence of other bodies such as Venus and Earth.

While Leverrier was preparing tables of Mercury's motions, he discovered that, in only 100 years, the planet's perihelion had precessed about 40 seconds more than it should have.

Leverrier, who located the planet Neptune from just such precise calculations, was convinced that an unknown planet, orbiting the Sun inside Mercury's orbit, was to blame for the discrepancy. He and other astronomers began a telescope search for this unknown planet, which they named Vulcan. Despite false alarms over a number of years, no such planet was found.

Eventually, physicists realized that if there was another planet large enough to affect Mercury in this way, it would also have an effect on the orbits of Venus and Earth. No such effects existed, and the "hidden planet" theory went out the window. The solution did not surface until 1916, when Albert Einstein published his General Theory of Relativity.

Beyond Newton

According to Einstein, small bodies behave differently when they are very close to extremely large bodies. Mercury's odd precession could be explained by its closeness to the Sun. Newtonian physics hold good for most calculations within the Solar System, where relationships involving fairly weak gravitational fields are usual.

The accuracy of Einstein's calculations was tested under rigorous conditions in 1919. During a total eclipse of the Sun astronomers photographed stars which were usually barely visible. The experiment was designed to test whether space itself curved close to large bodies, as Einstein believed. If it did, then light would curve with it. Stars close to the Sun that could be seen during the eclipse should be displaced from their expected positions by a calculable amount.

Photographs were taken, and the stars' positions measured. They were displaced by exactly the amount that Einstein had expected. This evidence showed the correctness of Einstein's mathematical calculations which explained the precession of Mercury's perihelion. Mercury had provided perhaps the very first example of the new physics in action.

The Sun in relation to the rest of the Solar System. It is many times larger than all its orbiting planets put together. It consists of almost 99·9 percent of all the material present in the Solar System.

PLUTO
NEPTUNE
URANUS
SATURN
JUPITER
MARS
EARTH
VENUS
MERCURY

The Sun

Of all the heavenly bodies that weave their complicated patterns across the sky, the Sun is by far the most dependable, and it was the most reassuring for the early sky-watchers. Every morning, it dispels the darkness. Every day, it follows its arc from east to west across the sky. The height and length of its solar journey vary with the seasons, as does the amount of warmth and light radiated, but the Sun never lets you down. It always turns up again in the morning. Even when the sky is covered with cloud, the Sun's light comes through even when the Sun's disk is obscured.

An Ordinary Star

The Sun occupies a unique and essential position in our lives. Perhaps the most astonishing thing scientists have discovered about it, then, is that it is quite ordinary. The Sun, it turns out, is an ordinary star, one of

Photographed by Skylab 3 using ultraviolet apparatus, this image reveals a solar eruption of gigantic size compared to Earth, which is pictured as a small dot for comparison.

SIZE OF EARTH

like thousands of millions in our Milky Way galaxy. We only know one thing about the Sun that sets it apart from the other stars we have observed. It is orbited by a family of planets.

So far, scientists have not managed to observe planets around any of the other stars upon which they have focused their telescopes. From what we know of

This color-coded image of the Sun indicates the regions of greatest ultraviolet / X-ray intensity as white, followed by yellow, red, pink and blue. Dark areas are "coronal holes," which are regions of low temperature, pressure, and magnetic field strength.

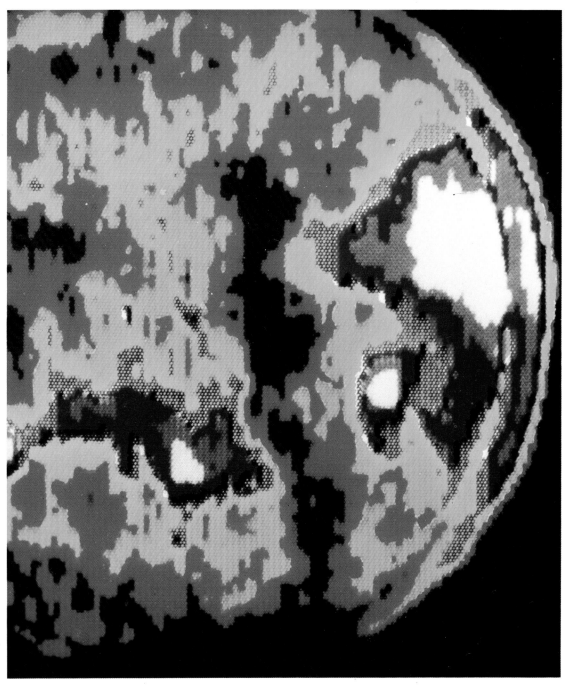

The Sun is a multi-layered body of different gases. In the permanent thermonuclear reaction at its core, hydrogen is converted to helium at enormous pressure and temperature. The photosphere, which is the outer layer under the chromosphere and corona of the solar atmosphere, is only 62 miles (100 kilometers) deep.

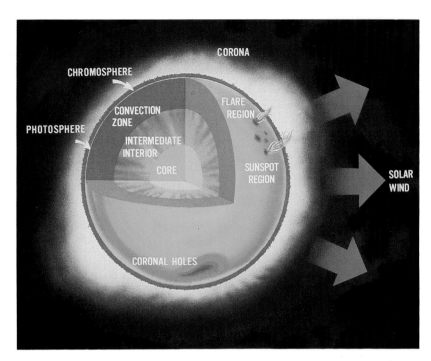

the way our Solar System was formed, there is a good chance that there are other planetary systems in space. There is no reason to think that the gases and elements that were the building blocks of our Sun and its planets could not behave in a similar way again during star formation. Perhaps they have, millions of times, in the existence of our galaxy alone.

The most probable reason why we have not yet seen other planetary systems is that even the nearest stars are huge distances away. The star nearest to us after the Sun is more than 250,000 times as far from us as the Sun. Remember, the Sun is 93,000,000 miles (150,000,000 kilometers) away from Earth. Also, compared to stars, planets are tiny and hard to see.

Solar Mass

The Sun contains about 99·9 percent of the entire mass of our Solar System. That leaves just over one tenth of one percent for all the planets, moons, asteroids, comets, meteors, and interplanetary dust and gas. This almost perfect sphere of hot gases has a diameter of 846,000 miles (1,360,000 kilometers).

There is an enormous range of temperature within the Sun. At the surface, which is whitish-yellow to our eyes (though we must be very careful never to look at it directly), the temperature is at its lowest, at around 5,800 K. K stands for *Kelvin*, a measure often used to record very high and very low temperatures.

Thermonuclear Fusion

At the Sun's core, the temperature is about 15,000,000 K. At the heart of this raging thermonuclear furnace, a sort of permanent hydrogen bomb explodes in slow motion. It converts 600,000,000 tons of hydrogen into helium every second, releasing energy at the same time. The Sun probably consists of about 92 percent hydrogen atoms, 7·8 percent helium atoms, and 0·2 percent atoms of heavier elements. With this amount of fuel, the Sun has a total active life of ten billion years. It has been blazing away for half that period already, so it is literally a middle-aged star. It has another five billion years to go.

Slow Birth of a Sunbeam

In the perpetual thermonuclear reactor at the Sun's core, that 600,000,000 tons of hydrogen is converted to 596 tons of helium and 4 tons of released energy. That energy is radiated slowly, over a period of two million years, toward the Sun's surface. To begin with, *photons* of electromagnetic radiation make this enormous and slow journey from the sun's center toward its surface by means of "radiative transfer." As they travel outward, they are transformed from mostly short-wavelength gamma rays, X-rays and ultraviolet rays, to

X-ray images from Skylab showed bright spots all over the Sun's surface. They have an average life of about 8 hours and are situated in regions of magnetic activity.

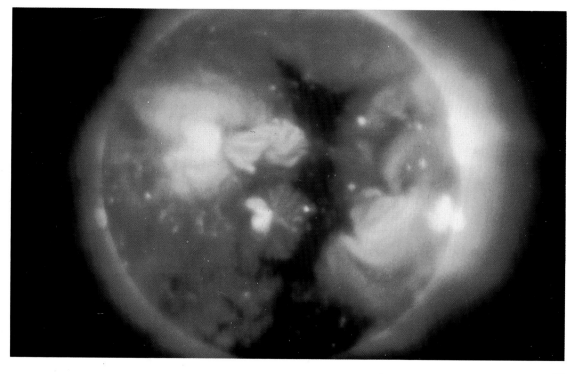

longer-wavelength radiation. This is fortunate for life on Earth, as a sunlight rich in gamma rays and X-rays would be fatal. About 125,000 miles (200,000 kilometers) from the Sun's surface, the energy radiated from the core starts to move in turbulent *convection currents*.

The outer layers of the Sun, known as the "solar atmosphere," consist of three regions. These are the *photosphere*, from which most of the Sun's radiated light comes; the *chromosphere*, a more volatile layer at higher altitude; and the *corona*. This outer region of very thin gases extends hundreds of thousands of miles from the photosphere.

Boiling Surface

An ordinary photograph of the Sun taken through an optical telescope is an image of the photosphere. This surface layer of the Sun is something over 62 miles (100 kilometers) thick. The photosphere's surface is made up

In the future, huge solar energy-harnessing arrays for receiving microwaves, like the one shown in this conceptual illustration may be used together with specially-adapted satellites to help solve Earth's energy problems.

In these images of the solar eruption of June 10, 1973, taken with differing intensities of ultraviolet light emission, the eruption at the top extends distinctly outward from the solar surface. A more dispersed emission appears in the right-hand image.

almost entirely of seething *granules*. These are huge patches of gas convection, constantly churning in a boiling motion, and often 625 miles (1,000 kilometers) and more across. Hot gases rise at great speed in the bright center of the granule, overflow, and start to cool. They run back down the sides of the granule into the darker, cooler regions between the patches. The hot mix of high-temperature hydrogen and helium that forms the granules radiates the Sun's light and heat, which warms and lights our planet.

Above the photosphere is the much thicker layer of the chromosphere. About 5,000 miles (8,000 kilometers) thick, the chromosphere is the region of the gaseous spikes

31

known as *spicules*. These tapering stalks of hot gases can be 625 miles (1,000 kilometers) thick. They cover the sun's globe like a transparent, glowing forest. Each spicule may last only fifteen minutes. With temperatures up to 20,000 K, they shoot at a speed of 20 miles (32 kilometers) a second into the upper reaches of the chromosphere. There, they penetrate the lower levels of the corona, the immense outer envelope of the sun's atmosphere.

High-Altitude Heat

The temperature in the corona can reach 2,000,000 K at an altitude of 50,000 miles (80,000 kilometers)

The temperature of the Sun's atmosphere increases dramatically with altitude. Solar prominences can be seen arcing high above the Sun's surface, and the effects of solar flares can be felt as radio blackouts on faraway Earth.

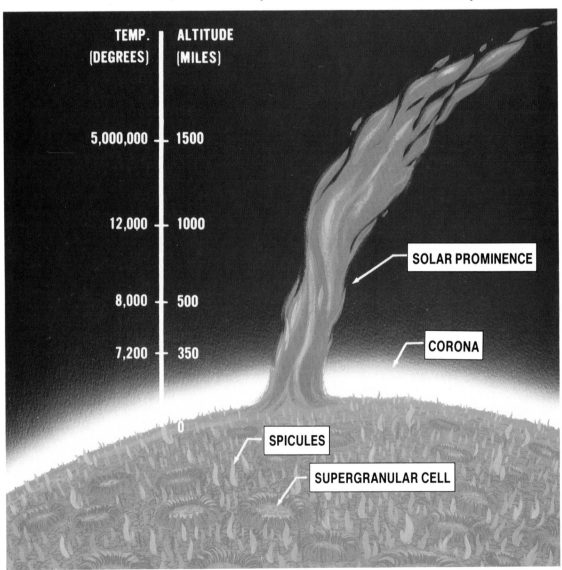

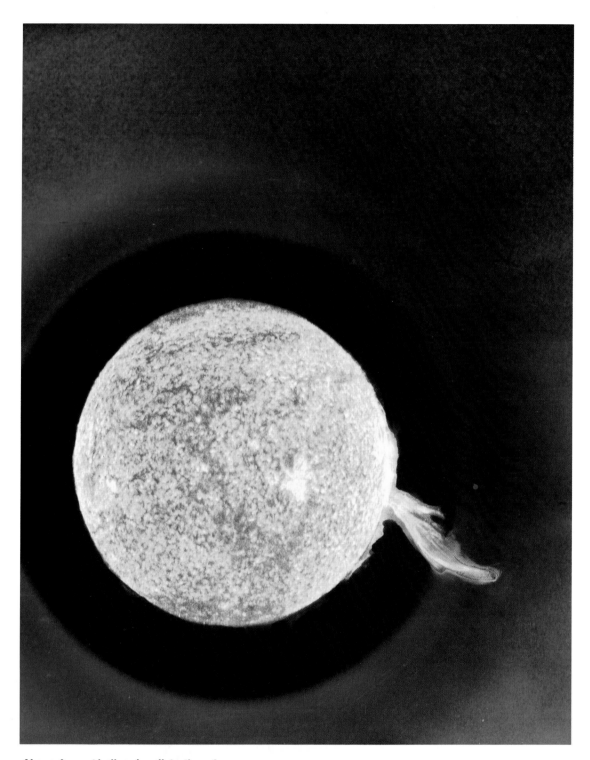

Above: A great ballooning distortion of
the Sun's corona, called a coronal
transient, is pushed out by the intense
activity in the eruptive prominence
which is itself as large as the radius of
the Sun.

above the photosphere. The corona changes shape according to the Sun's activity cycle. Sometimes, it is roughly symmetrical, with great streamers reaching out from its equatorial region. At other times, it is more evenly distributed around the Sun's globe.

Solar Eclipse

The corona is best seen on the rare occasion of a total solar eclipse. Then, the Moon is close to Earth and positioned in its orbit to lie exactly between the Earth and the Sun. On these occasions, the Moon, which is 400 times smaller than the Sun, but also 400 times

The temperature in the corona, imaged here by the Solar Max Satellite, increases with height, it can reach 4,000,000K.

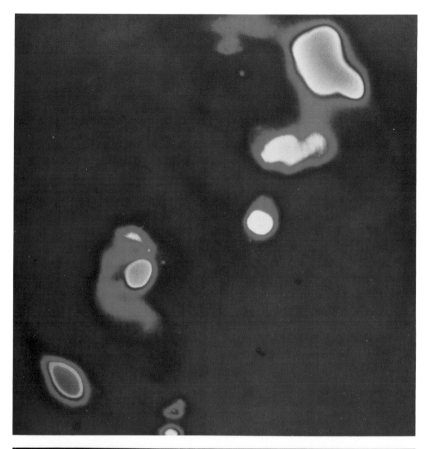

Skylab 2's X-ray telescope was used to take this brightness-image of high-temperature regions in the Sun's corona. White shows the brightest and hottest regions. Red indicates cooler areas.

Vega (arrowed), the third-brightest star in our sky and located in the Lyre constellation, is only one-fifth as old as our Sun, but it is twice its size and 60 times as luminous. Vega is 26 light-years from Earth and may be the center of a Solar System in the making.

A full solar eclipse by the Moon gives a clear view of the Sun's chromosphere, showing the distinct shape of a solar prominence rising above the red arc.

closer, completely obscures the main disk of the Sun. A total eclipse can only be seen from a narrow strip of the Earth's surface. It lasts, at the most, 7 minutes and 40 seconds and can be much less. For this brief period, the glowing shape of the corona can be seen radiating out from behind the dark disk of the moon. The corona

ECLIPSES IN THE 1990s

Date	Length of Totality	Where Visible
1991: Jul 11	7 minutes	Pacific, Central America, Brazil
1992: Jun 30	5½ minutes	South Atlantic
1994: Nov 3	4½ minutes	Peru, Brazil, South Atlantic
1995: Oct 24	2 minutes	Middle East, India, Pacific
1997: Mar 9	3 minutes	Soviet Union, Arctic
1998: Feb 24	4 minutes	Pacific, Central America, Atlantic
1999: Aug 11	2½ minutes	Atlantic, Europe, India

This solar eclipse of March 7, 1970, pictured from Miahuatlan in Mexico by scientists from the Houston Manned Spacecraft Center in Texas, shows the wide and irregular shape of the Sun's corona.

can extend out into space for several times the Sun's photospheric diameter.

Because total solar eclipses are few and far between, astronomers create an artificial eclipse, using an instrument called a coronograph, to study the corona.

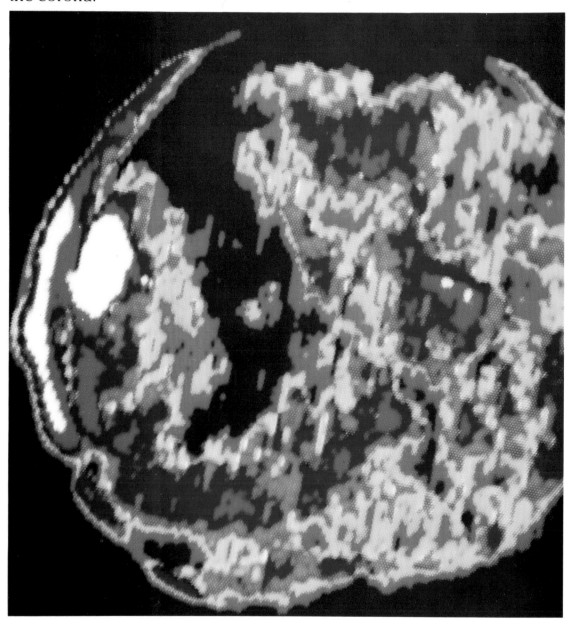

The coronal hole, seen in this Skylab image as a dark area, rotates along with the Sun, changing position from day to day. Coronal holes are regions of extremely low density and temperature in comparison with their surroundings. They may be the major source of the solar wind.

NASA's Orbiting Solar
Observatory 6 produced
this multicolored image of
the solar eclipse of March
7, 1970. OSO-6's ultraviolet
Spectral Heliograph
collected the data, which is
used to study the
ultraviolet emissions of the
Sun.

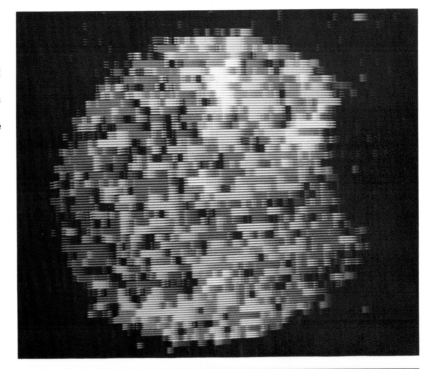

This false-color image of
the Sun's corona was
taken from Skylab. It
shows the range of
temperatures in the
various regions. The
hottest areas appear as
white.

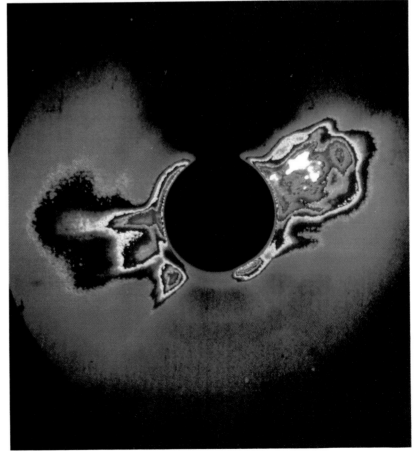

Sunspots and Solar Flares

Ordinary white-light photographs of the Sun usually reveal the dark patches of *sunspots*. They show sunspots to have a dark inner area, called the *umbra*, and a surrounding, lighter area, called the *penumbra*.

Sunspot activity seems to follow a cycle of about eleven years. At the time of most intensive activity, the photosphere of the Sun can be speckled with literally hundreds of sunspots. Over five or six years, the number is reduced to "sunspot minimum." Then, the photosphere's disk is sometimes completely clear. The activity then begins to build again, until "sunspot maximum" is reached once more.

Reaching out to the Sun

Because the Earth's atmosphere distorts our view of

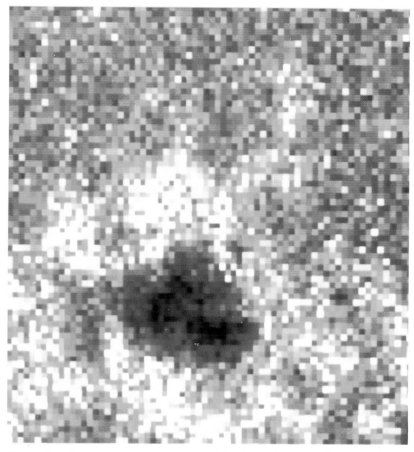

This sunspot was imaged by Solar Max's UV Spectrometer and Polarimeter. The spot is dark, with bright surrounding areas of increased temperature. This complete image covers an area 100,000 miles (160,000 kilometers) across.

the Sun's surface, some of the best observations have been made from high-altitude balloons. They carry telescopes and cameras 80,000 feet (25,000

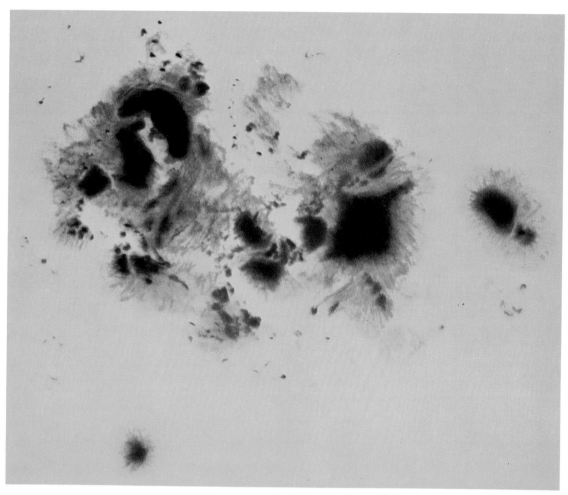

This large sunspot group was photographed in May, 1951, from Mount Wilson Observatory in California. The sunspot cycle had peaked in 1947.

meters) above our planet. The pictures taken from these high-floating observatories show tremendous detail.

Differential Rotation

A sunspot begins life as a small "pore." Over a period of a couple of weeks it may grow into a huge patch tens of thousands of miles across. Then, it starts to fade away once more. By observing sunspots, astronomers can calculate the Sun's rotational speed. Unlike the solid, terrestrial planets, the Sun, which is totally gaseous, has *differential rotation*. At the sun's equator, a sunspot makes a complete rotation to return to where it started in about 25 days. However, spots at higher latitudes take longer to make a full rotation. At latitude 90°, a rotation takes about 27½ days.

Sunspots appear dark to us because they are cooler than the surrounding bright photosphere – as much as 3,600°F (2,000°C) cooler. Scientists think that sunspots are caused by the Sun's differential rotation. As the Sun rotates, the lines of force of its magnetic field, which lie below the photosphere, are wound around it in an increasingly distorted manner. This twisting intensifies the magnetic field, and "loops" of magnetic pressure burst through the Sun's surface. At the points where the two "feet" of a loop break the surface, two associated sunspots of opposite magnetic *polarity* occur.

Reversing the Poles

As sunspots are produced, their strong, localized magnetic fields, the *polarities* of which are reversed on opposite sides of the Sun's equator, tend to cancel each other out at low latitudes and build up a weak general magnetic field at high atitudes. The polarities of this general magnetic field reverse every eleven years or so, following a reversal in the polarities of new sunspots on both sides of the Sun's equator. Therefore, the whole cycle is really 22 years, from one polarity, to its reverse, and then back to the original again.

Although sunspots show on the surface of our Sun, their strong magnetic fields reach deep into it. Like most moving magnetic fields, those of sunspots generate electricity. This force is sometimes discharged in a huge arc that can reach far out into the corona and last

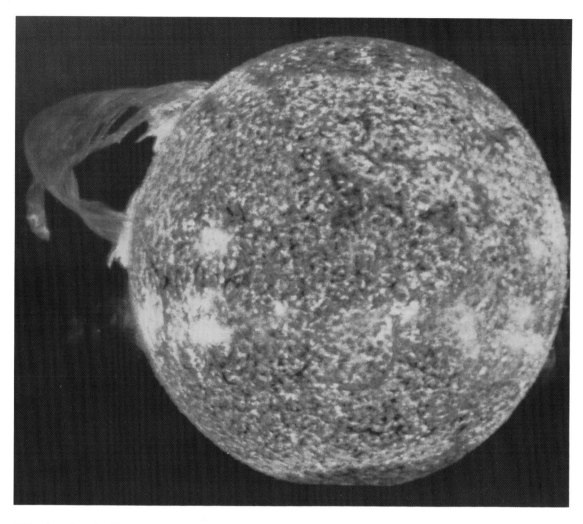

This gigantic solar flare, photographed by the earth-orbiting Skylab 4 on December 19, 1973, made an arc 367,000 miles (588,000 kilometers) across. The image was taken in the light of ionized helium. The Sun's poles (top and bottom) show up relatively darker and less granular than most of the surface.

for hours. These arc discharges are known as *solar flares*.

Selective Viewing

Astronomers have found that ordinary "white light" photographs of the Sun do not show all aspects of solar activity. Many events such as solar flares can be seen only by viewing the Sun in other wavelengths. Using an instrument with a "monochromatic" filter, scientists can block out all light except that emitted at a chosen wavelength. Photographs taken at certain wavelengths of light emitted by the high-temperature hydrogen atoms or calcium atoms above the Sun's "surface" or photosphere show the Sun's chromosphere. Solar flares come into sharp detail. It also becomes possible to distinguish the bright upper areas known as *plages* and the dark areas called *filaments*.

43

Eruptive solar events occur when the material breaks free from the magnetic "loop" holding it. The eruption is violent, flinging material many thousands of miles out from the solar disk.

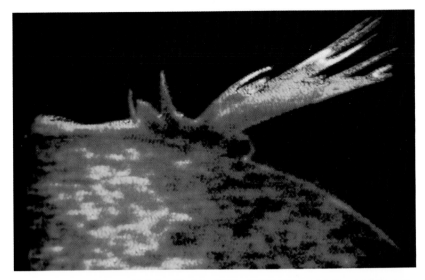

Above areas of strong solar activity, high temperature gases are kept in check by loops of magnetic energy.

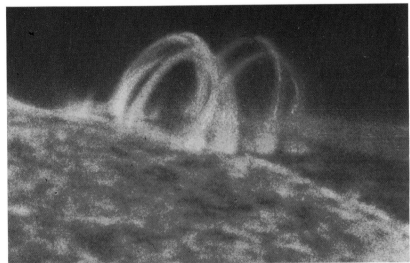

Originally taken in black and white in infrared light, this color image of a solar eruption has been electronically processed. The original picture was taken by Skylab 3's *spectro-heliograph*. At this stage, the solar eruption is 200,000 miles (322,000 kilometers) long.

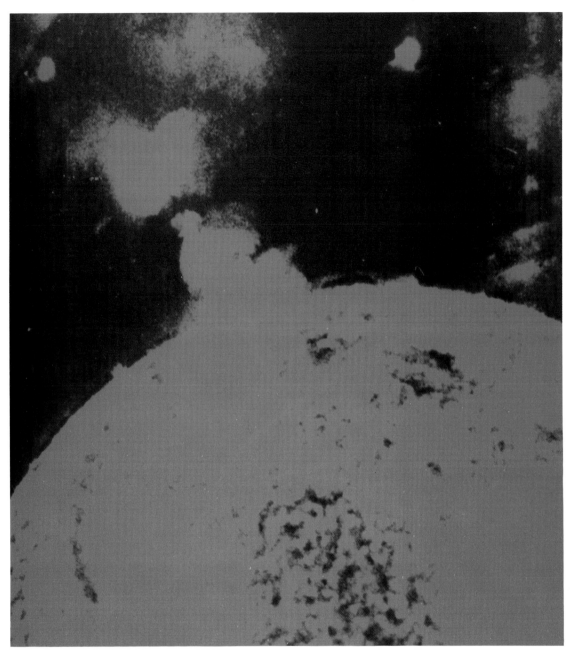

Solar eruptions emit clouds of charged particles capable of disrupting radio transmissions on Earth and sending magnetic navigational systems haywire. A U.S. Navy's research rocket carried the camera that took this picture in November, 1969.

Photographs taken at X-ray wavelengths reveal bright turbulence as strong magnetic fields burst out from the Sun's interior. This activity creates solar flares, which contribute to the enormously high temperatures of the corona, which can reach 2,000,000 K, compared to the photosphere's "surface" temperature of around 5,800 K.

The regular cycles of solar activity result in fluctuations in the emission of ultraviolet radiation and X-rays

45

and in the number of electrically charged particles that leave the Sun and travel through space as *solar wind*. As a result, solar cycles affect physical events on Earth, such as electromagnetic activity in the atmosphere and weather patterns.

Meteorologists have established that during "sunspot maxima," at the peak of sunspot activity, the Sun emits more radiation. This can cause relatively high

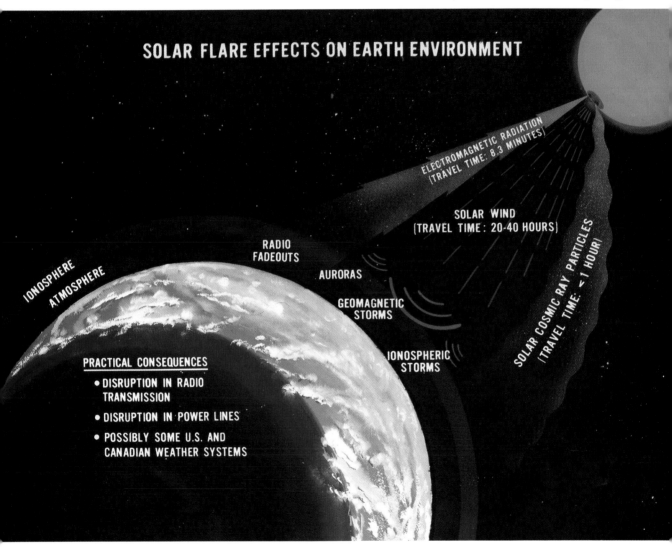

SOLAR FLARE EFFECTS ON EARTH ENVIRONMENT

ELECTROMAGNETIC RADIATION
(TRAVEL TIME: 8.3 MINUTES)

SOLAR WIND
(TRAVEL TIME: 20-40 HOURS)

SOLAR COSMIC RAY PARTICLES
(TRAVEL TIME: < 1 HOUR)

IONOSPHERE
ATMOSPHERE

RADIO
FADEOUTS

AURORAS

GEOMAGNETIC
STORMS

IONOSPHERIC
STORMS

PRACTICAL CONSEQUENCES

- DISRUPTION IN RADIO TRANSMISSION
- DISRUPTION IN POWER LINES
- POSSIBLY SOME U.S. AND CANADIAN WEATHER SYSTEMS

Periods of intense solar activity create dramatic aurora displays on Earth, as well as blacking out long-range radio transmissions. They can also seriously disturb the orbits of artificial satellites.

temperatures during midwinter in North America and mid-Europe. NASA's Solar Max satellite, launched in 1980, monitored the Sun's radiation very accurately. It measured the increase and decrease in brightness as sunspots built up and then faded over the 11-year cycle.

Little Ice Age

Scientists have built up historical records that give a

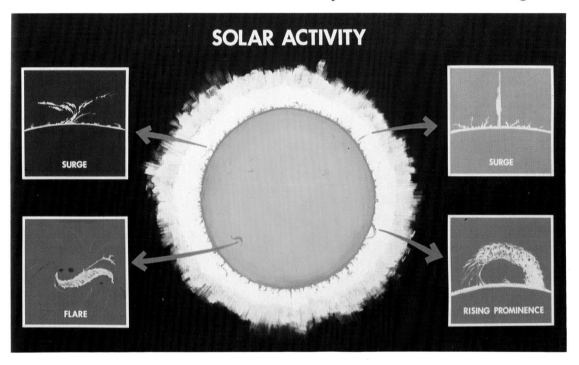

SOLAR ACTIVITY

SURGE

SURGE

FLARE

RISING PROMINENCE

Skylab's instruments were able to "see" several forms of solar activity by gathering information in several areas of the solar radiation spectrum, including the ultraviolet, X-ray, white light, and hydrogen-alpha bands.

full picture of sunspot activity back to the beginning of the seventeenth century. Between 1645 and 1715, there was a period of extremely low activity. To all intents and purposes, the Sun's magnetic cycle disappeared. That period, called the "Maunder minimum" after the astronomer who discovered it, was characterized by exceptionally cold winters, when rivers froze throughout Europe. In London, "frost fairs" were held on the thick ice that covered the River Thames, and the period has also become known as the "Little Ice Age."

Solar Storms

Exceptional solar flare activity can have startling effects on Earth. In February, 1942, during World War II, Allied coastal radar stations on the English Channel failed to intercept German battleships slipping through to their home ports, because solar flares had jammed the radar receivers. In March, 1989, a huge sequence of solar flares deluged the Earth with charged particles. They caused power surges in electricity supply grids in the northern United States and Canada, resulting in burned-out transformers and blacked-out cities.

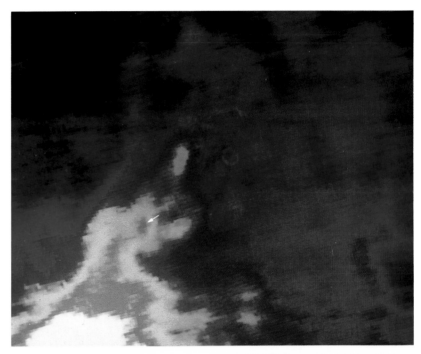

The Sun is a typical star. The arrow indicates a newborn protostar only about 100,000 years old, which is probably about the same size as our own Sun. It is situated in the Bernard 5 gas cloud in the Perseus constellation in the Milky Way, 1,000 light-years from Earth.

This Skylab ultraviolet image shows a solar prominence reaching out hundreds of thousands of miles beyond the Sun's disk. The coloring of the picture was achieved by enhancing black and white images by computer to emphasize differences in brightness.

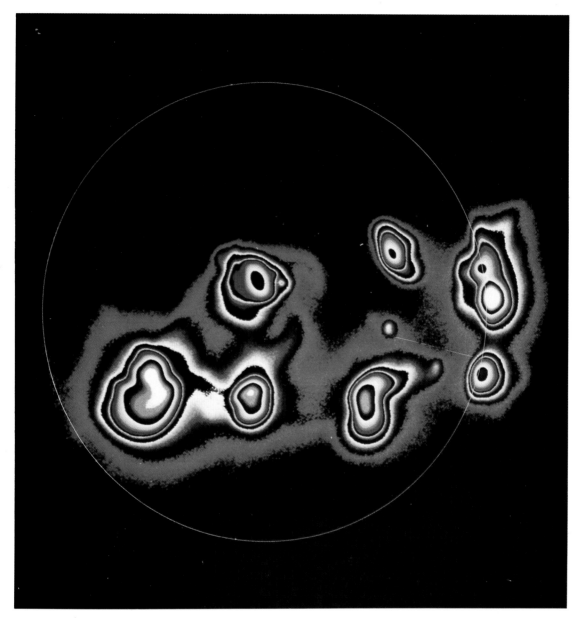

Auroras

The same solar magnetic storm caused spectacular *auroras* visible from high Earth latitudes. Charged particles flooded the "shock front" of our planet's own magnetosphere. They evaded the protective *Van Allen* radiation belt and poured down into the polar atmosphere to react with atoms and molecules there. The Earth's magnetosphere is shaped like a doughnut. The "holes" occur over the magnetic poles and let in solar particles. The results are the sheets of brilliant color displayed by the Northern and Southern Lights.

On each side of the Sun's equator is a belt known as a Region of Most Violent Activity. These areas appear at the beginning of each 11-year solar cycle at 45° latitude and gradually move in toward the equator.

An Expensive Business

The great solar magnetic storm of March, 1989, also had a dire effect on a large number of artificial satellites in a variety of Earth orbits. About 5,000 satellites were lost. Some strayed out of their orbits because of increased "drag" in the Earth's atmosphere as it was heated up and expanded by solar flare energy. Weather and survey satellites were the most vulnerable,

The bright solar flares visible (bottom left) on this NASA telescopic photograph, taken in August, 1972, was 100,000 miles (160,000 kilometers) across. It released energy equivalent to the entire electricity consumption of the United States for 100 million years.

since they must stay in very precise orbits to do their jobs. The early return of the Skylab space station in 1979 was partly due to solar flare drag in Earth's atmosphere. Solar activity can be an expensive business. The Solar Maximum Mission satellite (Solar Max), which carried out valuable measurements and surveys of the Sun in the 1980s, itself became a victim of upper atmosphere solar flare drag. It plummeted to Earth on December 2, 1989, ahead of schedule.

Tree Ring Records

Written records show that the earliest telescopic viewings of sunspot activity were made in 1610. However, naked-eye observations are recorded at least as early as the 4th century B.C. Scientists have discovered another method of looking back at solar activity in historical times: they study the growth rings of ancient but still living trees. Plants, as they use sunlight, absorb certain forms of carbon. These include an *isotope* of carbon called C-14. The amount of C-14 in the Earth's atmosphere is governed by cosmic rays from outside the Solar System. Solar activity regulates the penetration of these rays. High C-14 levels in plant structure reflect low levels of solar activity.

Examination of bristlecone pines, some of the oldest living organisms on Earth, reveal that, since 3,000 B.C., there have been six periods of strong activity, and six of almost no activity. The Maunder minimum was one such calm. There was a period of high activity between A.D. 1100 and 1250, which may have created favorable conditions for the Vikings to explore Greenland and North America. So solar activity may even affect important historical events on Earth.

Storm Watch

The U.S. Space Environment Service Center keeps a constant watch on solar activity. It issues warnings whenever magnetic storms and flares pose a threat to earthly power grids, long-range communication networks, and scheduled space flights. Since the 1970's, the U.S.S.R. has been monitoring solar radiation from a sequence of Prognoz spacecraft launched into high elliptical orbits. Most of the Prognoz craft take about 4 days to orbit the Earth. They come as close as 300 miles (483 kilometers) from Earth at *perigee* and go as far as 125,000 miles (200,000 kilometers) away at *apogee*. They have been particularly useful to the Soviet manned space program, warning of periods when there may be danger from solar activity.

Opposite: The satellite Orbiting Solar Observatory 7 took this ultraviolet image of the Sun in August, 1972. White regions indicate an enormous solar storm in action. On Earth, electricity supply systems were affected by this super-storm.

At the center of this image, is the edge-on disk of what could be another Solar System, 50 light-years from Earth. The star at the center of the disk, composed of ice, carbon, and silicate material, is called Beta Pictoris.

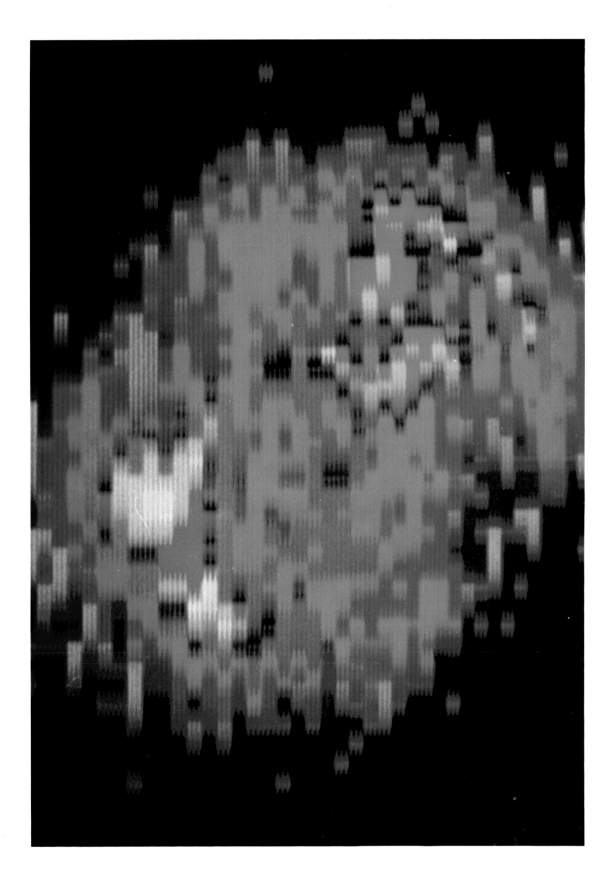

The Solar Wind

In addition to the deluges of charged particles that rush across space following the explosion of a solar flare, there is a much more steady and constant stream of particles known as the *solar wind*.

The charged particles of the solar wind spray in a spiral away from the Sun in all directions, like water

Particles from solar flares reach Earth in a matter of hours. Satellite monitors now give early warnings so that Earth stations can be ready for the disruptive effects of such massive energy releases.

from a rotating sprinkler. The solar wind consists of atoms and *ions* (an atom or molecule with either a positive or negative electrical charge). These particles speed so fast through the Sun's corona that they escape the Sun's gravity. In a way, the solar wind is an extension of the corona: anything that it touches out in space is technically within the Sun's atmosphere.

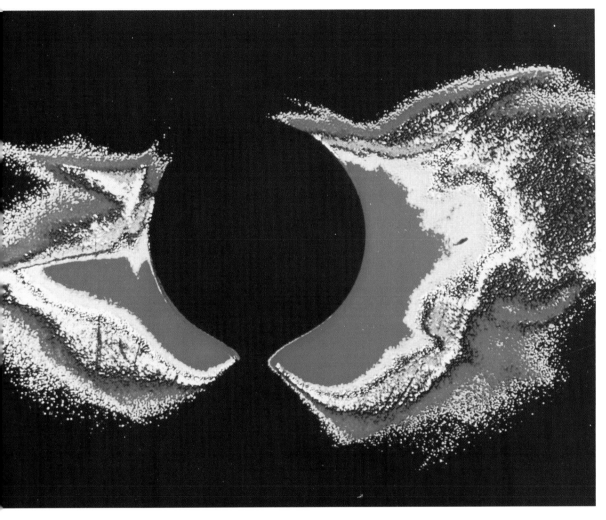

By creating an artificial eclipse of the Sun with the aid of a coronagraph, Skylab has been able to take a clear picture of the solar corona, color-coded for differences in bright- ness. It extends millions of miles from the Sun's disk.

Catching the Wind

The Soviet Luna 3 space probe first detected the solar wind in 1959, followed by NASA's Explorer 10 in 1961. The first properly equipped observations of the solar wind came from Mariner 2, on its way to Venus in 1962. Mariner 2 confirmed that there was a constant flow of *protons* and *electrons* (positive and negative elementary particles) away from the Sun. Their speeds vary between 220 and 500 miles (350 and 800 kilometers) per second. The mix of "ionized" particles is called a "*plasma*."

When comets pass near the Sun, we can see the effects of the solar wind. It always blows the comet's tail away from the Sun, like a flag in the breeze. The solar wind has a similar "tailing" effect on the magnetic

At the distant edge of the solar corona, streamers of energy, caught in this X-ray and ultraviolet image from Skylab's Solar Telescope, reach out into space.

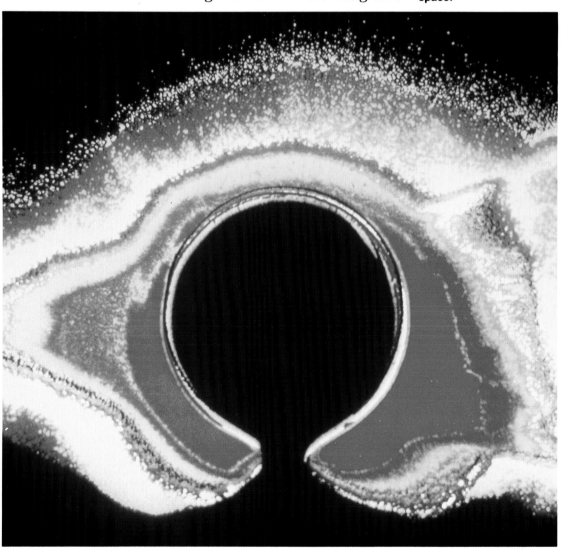

field, or "magnetosphere," of the Earth. Mariner 2 discovered that, where the solar wind met the magnetosphere, it created a bow-shaped shockwave. On the other side of the Earth, the magnetosphere was blown out into a long, trailing tail. The supersonic wind is extremely hot (between 50,000 and 500,000 K), and has a very low density – Mariner 2 found just 150 particles per cubic inch (9 per cubic centimeter).

The constant solar wind strips the Sun of a million tons of hydrogen every second. Yet even after ten billion years, only one-billionth of the Sun's mass will have disappeared this way.

The illustration below shows the various craft that may be employed to gain information about the magnetosphere.

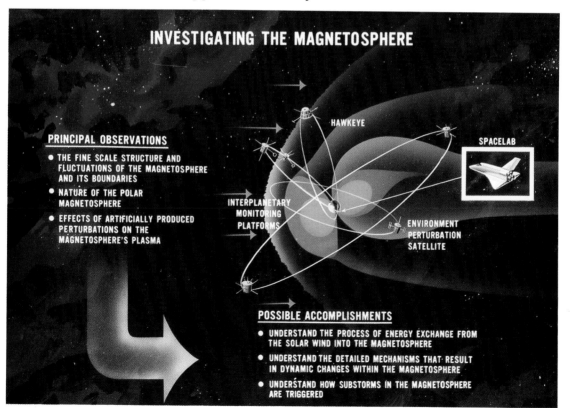

INVESTIGATING THE MAGNETOSPHERE

HAWKEYE

SPACELAB

PRINCIPAL OBSERVATIONS

- THE FINE SCALE STRUCTURE AND FLUCTUATIONS OF THE MAGNETOSPHERE AND ITS BOUNDARIES
- NATURE OF THE POLAR MAGNETOSPHERE
- EFFECTS OF ARTIFICIALLY PRODUCED PERTURBATIONS ON THE MAGNETOSPHERE'S PLASMA

INTERPLANETARY MONITORING PLATFORMS

ENVIRONMENT PERTURBATION SATELLITE

POSSIBLE ACCOMPLISHMENTS

- UNDERSTAND THE PROCESS OF ENERGY EXCHANGE FROM THE SOLAR WIND INTO THE MAGNETOSPHERE
- UNDERSTAND THE DETAILED MECHANISMS THAT RESULT IN DYNAMIC CHANGES WITHIN THE MAGNETOSPHERE
- UNDERSTAND HOW SUBSTORMS IN THE MAGNETOSPHERE ARE TRIGGERED

The Neutrino Telescope

The oddest of all the instruments used to observe solar activity is the *neutrino* telescope. It is not a telescope at all in the usual sense of the word, but a huge tank full of dry-cleaning fluid, 100,000 gallons of it, buried a mile deep in a gold mine in South Dakota. Among the by-products of the process in which hydrogen changes to helium in the Sun's core are very unusual particles called *neutrinos*. They travel at great speed and pass with ease through most solids. They pass through the Earth, and through nearly everything on it, including ourselves. However, chlorine atoms can "catch" neutrinos. The neutrino telescope tank contains

The neutrino "telescope" – a huge tank of cleaning fluid – at Homestake Mine, South Dakota, traps neutrino particles as they hurtle from the Sun at the speed of light.

perchloroethylene, a cleaning fluid rich in chlorine atoms. A chlorine atom that catches a neutrino changes into an argon atom, so scientists at the gold mine can estimate the number of neutrinos produced by the Sun by regularly counting argon atoms in the tank.

Looking into the Future

The number of neutrinos should give an indication of the level of energy formation in the Sun's core. Because the neutrino flashes out of the core and across space at the speed of light, it tells us the state of the Sun's core right now. Calculations seem to show that the current rate of production of heat and energy at the core is considerably less than the heat and activity going on at the surface would need. However, what we see and measure at the surface has taken millions of years to travel from the core. Therefore, it is possible that the neutrinos are telling us that in a few million years, the Sun will go through a phase of much reduced heat and activity. This could be part of a very long-term cycle. Perhaps the same sequence of heating and cooling was responsible for the ice ages in the past.

Only Five Billion Years to Go

Scientists believe they can predict with accuracy how the Solar System will come to an end. This event is so far away that it is pointless to worry about it. The Sun is about halfway through its life as a steadily shining, planet-orbited star. It will continue, much as it is now, for another five billion years. By that time, it will have used up its hydrogen supply. Then, the core will contract, and the main body of the Sun will begin to swell. It will grow so large that it will swallow up all the inner planets, including the Earth. Long before the expanding *"red giant"* consumes the planet itself, the atmosphere, water, and all life on Earth will have evaporated in the increasing heat.

Eventually, the Sun will burn up all its helium and collapse inward to become a *"white dwarf"* star, hardly bigger than the Earth.

Books to Read

INTRODUCTORY READING

Cosmic Countdown: What Astronomers Have Learned about the Life of the Universe
   by Francine Jacobs (M Evans, 1988)
How Did We Find Out About the Universe? by Isaac Asimov (Walker & Co., 1983)
How our Universe Works by Al Snyder (Snyder Institute of Research, 1978)
Mercury: The Quick Planet by Isaac Asimov (Gareth Stevens Inc., 1989)
Mysteries of the Universe by Franklyn M. Branley (Lodestar Books, 1984)
The Mysterious Universe by Robin Kerrod (Lerner Publications, 1986)
The Origin and Evolution of Our Own Particular Universe
   by David E. Fisher (Macmillan, 1988)
Our Amazing Sun by Richard Adams (Troll Associates, 1983)
The Sun by Heather Couper & Nigel Henbest (Franklin Watts, 1987)
The Sun by Christopher Lampton (Franklin Watts, 1982)
The Sun by Kate Petty (Franklin Watts, 1985)
Sun and Stars by Norman Barrett (Franklyn Watts, 1986)
The Sun: Our Nearest Star by Franklyn M. Branley (Harper & Row Junior Books, 1988)
The Sun: Our Neighborhood Star by David J. Darling (Dillon Press, 1984)
Universe, The: Past, Present and Future by David J. Darling (Dillon Press, 1985)

FURTHER READING

Earthlike Planets: Surfaces of Mercury, Venus, Earth, Moon, Mars
   by Bruce Murray, et al (W. H. Freeman, 1981)
Exploring Solar Energy: Principles and Projects by Allan Kaufman (Prakken, 1989)
Fire of Life: The Smithsonian Book of the Sun
   Introduced by S. Dillon Ripley (W. W. Norton, 1981)
Interiors of the Planets by A. H. Cook (Cambridge University Press, 1981)
Introduction to Planetary Geology by Billy P. Glass (Cambridge University Press, 1982)
Mercury: The Elusive Planet by Robert G. Strom (Smithsonian Institution Press, 1987)
A Photographic Atlas of the Planets by Geoffrey Briggs & Frederic Taylor
   (Cambridge University Press, 1986)
Solar Energy – Simplified by Frank L. Bouquet (Systems Co., 1988)
Sun by Patrick Moore (W. W. Norton, 1968)
The Sun by Time-Life Book Editors (Time-Life, 1990)
Sun Up to Sun Down: Understanding Solar Energy by Shawn Buckley (McGraw-Hill, 1979)
Sunspots by R. J. Bray & R. E. Loughhead (Dover Press, 1979)
Sunspots, Dust and Rainfall by George N. Newhall (S&G Publishing, 1988)
Universe Guide to Stars and Planets by Ian Ridpath & Wil Tirion (Universe Books, 1985)
The View from Space: Photographic Exploration of the Planets
   by Merton Davies & Bruce C. Murray (Columbia University Press, 1971)

Glossary

APHELION The point in a planets orbit when it is farthest from the Sun.

APOGEE The farthest point from Earth of anything in orbit around it.

ASTEROID One of the thousands of minor planets in the Solar System, mainly less than 60 miles (100 kilometers) in diameter.

AURORA A display of light radiated by charged particles in a planet's upper atmosphere, usually over the magnetic poles.

AXIS An imaginary line through the center of a body, often a central line of rotation.

CHROMOSPHERE The 5,000 miles (8,000 kilometers) thick layer of solar atmosphere above the photosphere and below the corona.

CONVECTION CURRENTS Cyclical movements of gases or liquids caused by heating and cooling.

CORONA The Sun's outer atmospheric layer of thin gases. It extends hundreds of thousands of kilometers out into space.

DIFFERENTIAL ROTATION The way in which non-solid bodies rotate at different speeds at different latitudes.

ECCENTRIC ORBIT A non-circular orbit, usually an ellipse. The more eccentric the orbit, the "flatter" it is.

ELECTRON A negatively charged elementary particle.

ELLIPSE/ELLIPTICAL A shape adopted by non-circular planetary orbits, which is the section of a cone cut through by a plane.

ELONGATION The visible distance between two bodies in the sky seen from Earth, and expressed as an angle to Earth.

FILAMENTS Dark clouds of gas in the upper reaches of the Sun's chromosphere, which are at lower temperatures than their surroundings.

GRANULE Patches on the Sun's surface caused by pockets of gas continually rising and falling.

INFERIOR CONJUNCTION The position of a planet with an orbit smaller than Earth's, when it is in line between Earth and the Sun.

ION An atom or molecule electrically charged by having gainned or lost electrons.

ISOTOPE Forms of an element with the same number of protons in their nuclei, but different numbers of neutrons.

KELVIN SCALE A temperature scale with zero at absolute zero. 0 Kelvin $= -459 \cdot 6°F$ $(-273 \cdot 1°C)$.

MAGNETOMETER An instrument for measuring the strength and direction of a magnetic field.

MANTLE The layer beneath the crust of a planet.

NEUTRINO An elementary particle that travels at the speed of light.

PENUMBRA The larger, lighter area around the umbra of a sunspot.

PERIGEE The closest point to Earth of anything in orbit around it.

PERIHELION The point in a planet's orbit when it is closest to the Sun.

PHOTON An individually distinct unit of electromagnetic energy.

PHOTOSPHERE The visible surface layer of the Sun.

PLAGES Bright area of high temperature in the Sun's chromosphere.

PLASMA An ionized gas containing both ions and electrons.

POLARITY The north-south, positive-negative structure and orientation of magnetic force lines in a magnetic field.

PROTON An elementary particle with a positive charge which forms the nucleus of the hydrogen atom.

RADIO TELESCOPE An instrument with an antenna for picking up radio-frequency emissions from sources in space.

RED GIANT A star in one of its final phases, expanded into a huge shell of burning hydrogen with a helium core.

SILICON A natural, non-metallic element, the second most abundant element in the Earth's crust, after oxygen.

SOLAR FLARES Enormous releases of magnetic energy that erupt periodically from the Sun's chromosphere.

SOLAR WIND A plasma flow from the Sun radiating throughout the Solar System.

SPICULE Vertical gas jets in the Sun's chromosphere.

SUPERIOR CONJUNCTION The position of a planet with an orbit smaller than Earth's, aligned with Earth, but on the far side of the Sun.

TERRESTRIAL PLANET Any one of the four planets closest to the Sun: Mercury, Venus, Earth, and Mars.

TRANSIT The path of an inferior planet across the Sun's disk, or of a satellite across the disk of its planet.

VAN ALLEN RADIATION BELTS Two bands or charged particles trapped by Earth's magnetic field.

WHITE DWARF A collapsed, dying star that has burned most of its nuclear fuel.

ZENITH The point on the celestial sphere directly above an observer's head.

Looking at the Planets

The best time to look at Mercury is about 50 minutes before sunrise, or 50 minutes after sunset. When we look toward Mercury, the innermost planet, we are also looking in the direction of the Sun. It is very important not to look at the Sun directly.

Using binoculars or a telescope, seek Mercury out at the points in its orbit when it is farthest to one side of the Sun or the other, before sunrise or after sunset. An almanac will tell you whether this "point of greatest elongation," as it is called, is to the west (right) or east (left). If it is west, it will be a morning sighting. If it is east, Mercury will be visible in the evening. When you know the date, and on which side of the Sun to look, find a spot with a clear view of the horizon if possible. Search for the planet about a handspan away from where the Sun will be coming up or has already gone down. You will see a tiny pinkish shining object.

You may be able to see it for about two weeks before it is overwhelmed by the Sun's light. Six weeks later it will reappear on the opposite elongation.

Index